THE WAR OF SOAPS & SPONGES

W0391194

PHOEBE AKINTEYE

Hi, friend. Today I want to tell you a story about **soaps and sponges.**

You are probably wondering what all this will be about.

Well, I can assure you that you will enjoy this story every step of the way. Okay, let's get started.

On an amazing planet called **Earth**, early in the morning, nearly everyone was **happily having a shower**. And guess what? They were using soaps and sponges. This went on every day. People loved their bath time and shower time.

Then, **one dark day**, a little boy was about to have a **bubble** bath. He had already filled the bathtub. Suddenly, he started hearing **splashing and sploshing**.

The soap and the sponge he wanted to use had got sick of each other.

They were having a fight.

"Hey, Soap, did you know that you can't do anything without me? All you do is make the body smell nice. I do the best job here, I scrub all the dirt off," said Sponge.

“Well, you can’t do anything without me,” Soap argued.

The argument grew and there was a riot between all the soaps and sponges.

Then they split up.

One day, they were all invited to a party. When all of the sponges saw the soaps again, they started another fight.

"We are better than you," the sponges shouted. The king of the soaps was at the party and he decreed that "all of the soaps and sponges shall never see each other again."

That was the end of it. The sponges got angry and left the place called Cleanville. They went to a place called Lonely Land.

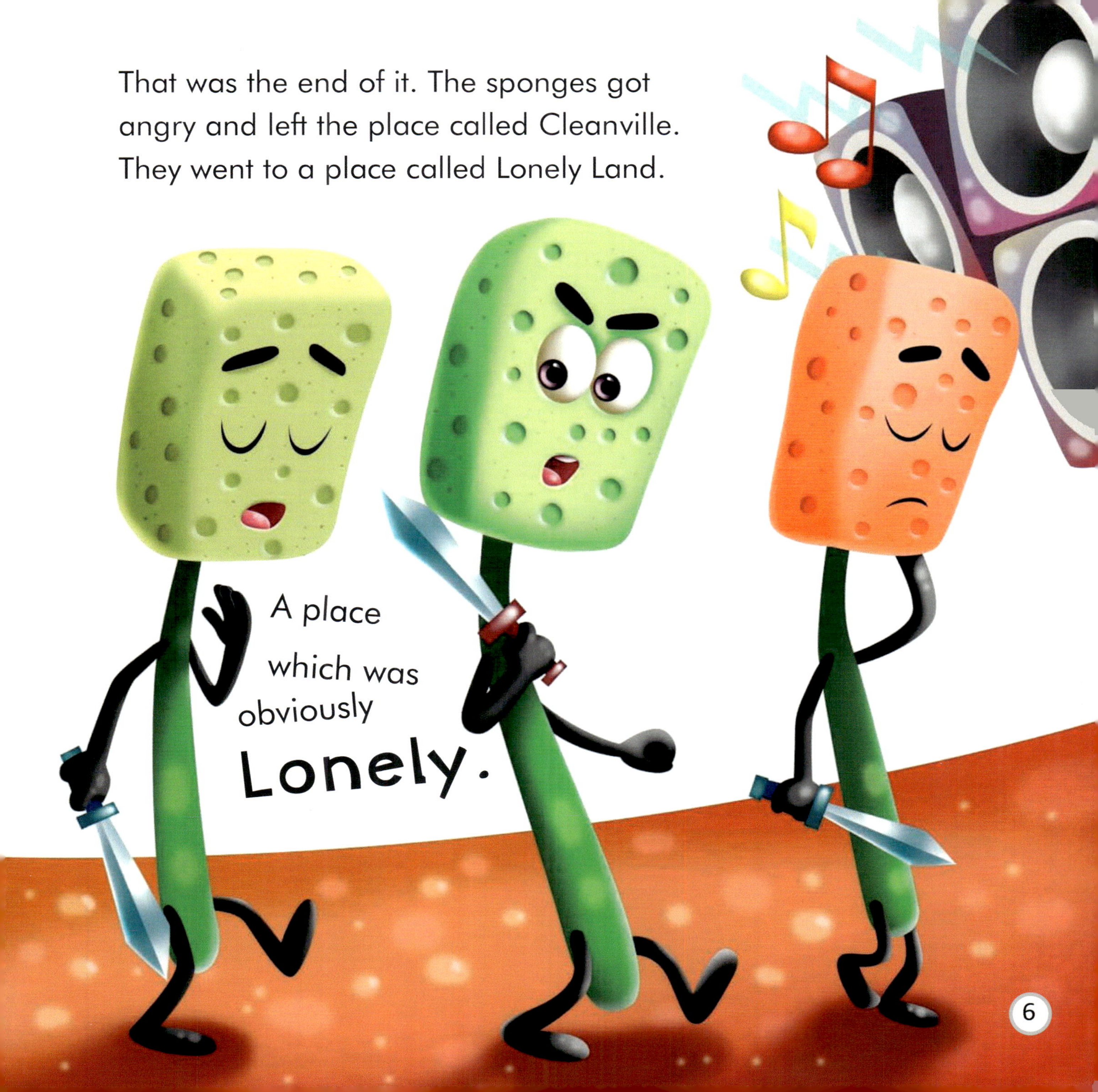

A place which was obviously **Lonely.**

Cleanville was no longer clean.

In fact, I would call it ***Stinkville.***

It stank badly because the soaps had left to go to a place called **Ego** Village. Everyone there was proud and full of themselves.

Many years passed and humans didn't have a **clue what soaps and sponges were!** All the people were smelly and dirty. They were full of mud and moles, and some of them were even **growing plants on their skin.**

Unbelievably, people were beginning to grow **mushrooms** on their noses, which was absolutely disgusting.

One day, a seven year old girl called **Detalina**, found a soap wandering about. She thought to herself, '**What is this?**'

When the soap saw Detalina, he wanted to run but she quickly caught up with him. "What are you called?" asked Detalina.

"I am ... a soap and I make ... bodies smell good. I also make them shine," the soap stuttered.

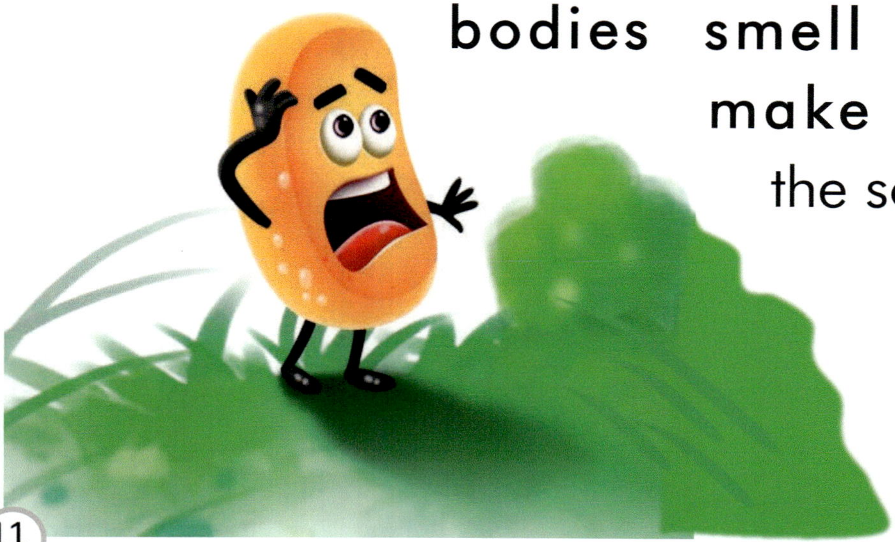

"How do you make our bodies shine?" Detalina asked.

"Well, you pick us up and rub us all over your body. It's as easy as ABC!" replied the soap.

"Ok, can I have a go?" She picked up the soap and rubbed it all over her face and arms. The soap told her to wash it off with water, so she did.

There was soap lather all over her.

Bubbles floated around her, too. She was amused and said, “**Wow!** What are these? They look amazing and I can **pop** them, too.”

The soap banged his head with his hand while shaking his head. "Duh, that is what soaps do. They bubble."

Then, when she smelt herself, she smelt like a rose. Detalina sniffed the beautiful rosy smell coming from her tough skin. "Can I keep this smell forever?" she asked.

The soap turned around and mumbled,

"You can keep the smell only if you have a shower or bath every day. Ahem, you'd need to look for a way to get rid of the mud, mushrooms, grass, and moles on your body." He walked away.

Detalina ran after him and said,

"Did you just say I should get rid of something? What should I get rid of?"

The soap ignored her and kept walking. Detalina ran after him again.

She picked him up and dunked him in a pail of water nearby, then rubbed him in the water with her hands, making loads of bubbles out of him.

"Repeat what you said," Detalina shouted angrily.

The soap screamed, "Help! Stop this. Don't make me dissolve in this water ... okay, okay, I surrender. Just get me out of this water and leave me alone."

"Fine!" said Detalina, "as long as you tell me what you said before."

"Alright!" the soap exclaimed. "I said that you need to get all of the moles, grass, mud, and mushrooms off your body."

"How am I supposed to do that?" Detalina asked.

"Well, you need sponges to do that job," the soap suggested as he walked away.

Detalina ran after him, "What are **sss-ssspp-sspeeengaass**, spengas?" she stuttered, looking confused.

"Sponges. They are called sponges, but don't ask me where they are because I don't know, ok? We are not on good terms. Well, we used to be, but many years ago a big argument broke out and we split up," the soap said. "**Alright**, I guess our conversation has to end here."

Detalina **moaned** sadly. Still, she was excited to go home and tell her parents about what had happened.

When Detalina got home, she ran to her parents and shouted, "Mum, Dad, guess what I saw today? I saw a creature called **soap**. He told me to pick him up and rub him all over my arms and face, then wash it off with water, which I did. I smelt myself after, and I smelt like a **rose**. You don't believe me, do you? Smell me for yourself."

Detalina spread out her arms.

"Mmmm, that smells divine.
Where do we get that smell?"
her parents wondered.

"But Mum, there is something I need to tell you. The soap said that all these things on our body can be removed. We need **sponges** to get rid of all the things on our skin. Unfortunately, the soap doesn't know where they are," Detalina explained.

"What do they look like? Is there any way we can make them?" Detalina's dad asked curiously.

"Well, we can try to find the soap. Come on, Mum and Dad, let's go look for him," said Detalina. They looked everywhere but he was far gone.

Some days later, Detalina and her parents found the soap and called out, “**Soap, stop and listen!** We need to talk to you. What does a sponge look like?”

"Uuuurrrrmmm, well, there are honeycomb sponges, mesh sponges, loofah sponges, and so on.

In short, there are lots of them. I am sorry but at this point, I cannot help you. On the bright side, I can take you to my leader because I believe he knows much more than I do."

After walking for **two** hours, they got to the leader of all soaps. When they arrived, they walked up to the leader. The soap said, "Leader, I am sorry, but the humans now know. They know everything. They even know about the sponges...

Leader, I apologise. Truly, I didn't want to tell them but they were terrorising and threatening me. I couldn't help it. Otherwise, they would hurt me more and I hated it," the frightened soap said.

"There is no need to apologise. **It has been too long**. We have been useless, worthless, and now we are ashamed of ourselves. Well, we will need to tell the humans about this sometime anyway.

But if we want to solve this problem, we will need to take a trip to Lonely Land. If we do, we will need to make peace with the sponges. Once we have done that, we can start doing what we do best with each other."

The next day, the king of the soaps and some other soaps started their journey to Lonely Land. Lonely Land was quite far, so it took them two days to get there. When they *finally* arrived, they went over to the king of sponges and said to him and all the sponges, "We know that you are still mad at us for what we did but we now come in peace...

We came mostly to say that we have been hidden and separated for too long. It is now time for us to start doing what we do best with each other, which is washing bodies and making things clean. The humans know already."

"I agree, it has been too long," said the sponge king. "We don't even know what to do with ourselves. It has been **lonely and boring** all these years. We can be friends again. I admit, we need each other." The soap king and the sponge king agreed.

"Let us move back to Cleanville. What are you waiting for?!" the kings announced at the same time. "**YES!**" the soaps and sponges exclaimed joyfully.

Back in Cleanville, Detalina had already told everyone about their acquaintance, the soap, and what he was doing to help.

Everyone went to the centre of town, waiting eagerly for the return of the soaps, and maybe the sponges, too.

This part of the story is my favourite.

When Detalina saw the soaps from afar, she was overjoyed. She shouted, **"That's them, they are here!"** All the people jumped happily and hugged each other. Detalina walked up to meet the soap and asked if the sponges were happy to come with them to Cleanville.

The soap looked sober and said, **"No."**

He was trying to trick Detalina. She looked disappointed and wanted to turn around to go back to her parents. Then the soap laughed out loud. "**I'm joking**. **They are here, too.** They are behind us." The soap pointed to them.

"YİPPEE!" everyone rejoiced.

One soap and one sponge went to each person. **"You can have us,"** they said to the humans.

"Everyone picked up their soaps and sponges. Then they went into their houses, got buckets of water, and started **scrubbing** their bodies.

Detalina started a song which everyone sang with her,

"Scrub my body yeah, yeah, scrub my body yeah, scrub my body yeah, yeah, scrub my body yeah."

They danced to the right and wiggled to the left as they had a good wash, scrubbing off all the dirt, moulds, and mushrooms on their bodies.

Bath time became a fun time for everyone. They sang the song over and over again.

I knew that you would enjoy the story.

"Scrub your body yeah, yeah, scrub your body yeah."

A little fight or an argument can destroy beautiful things, and this can go on for many years if not resolved. When there is misunderstanding, we should try to make peace before it becomes a bigger problem. We all need one another.

I hope you have enjoyed this story. 

From the author

PHOEBE

XXX